First World War
and Army of Occupation
War Diary
France, Belgium and Germany

41 DIVISION
Divisional Troops
Divisional Ammunition Column
6 March 1918 - 30 September 1919

WO95/2625/9

The Naval & Military Press Ltd
www.nmarchive.com
Published in association with The National Archives

Published by

The Naval & Military Press Ltd

Unit 10 Ridgewood Industrial Park,

Uckfield, East Sussex,

TN22 5QE England

Tel: +44 (0) 1825 749494

www.naval-military-press.com

www.nmarchive.com

This diary has been reprinted in facsimile from the original. Any imperfections are inevitably reproduced and the quality may fall short of modern type and cartographic standards.

© **Crown Copyright**
Images reproduced by permission of The National Archives, London, England, 2015.

Contents

Document type	Place/Title	Date From	Date To
Heading	WO95/2625/11 41 Div Div Amm'n Column March 1918 Sept 1919		
Heading	Vedelago	05/03/1918	05/03/1918
War Diary	Castagnole	06/03/1918	07/03/1918
War Diary	On Train	10/03/1918	11/03/1918
War Diary	Billets Nr Doullens	12/03/1918	21/03/1918
War Diary	Molliens-Au-Bois	22/03/1918	22/03/1918
War Diary	Achiet-Le-Grand	23/03/1918	23/03/1918
War Diary	Achiet-Le-Petit	24/03/1918	24/03/1918
War Diary	Bucquoy	24/03/1918	25/03/1918
War Diary	Nr. Essarts	25/03/1918	25/03/1918
War Diary	Souastre	26/03/1918	26/03/1918
War Diary	Berles-Au-Bois	27/03/1918	27/03/1918
War Diary	Souastre	28/03/1918	29/03/1918
Heading	41st Divisional Artillery War Diary 41st Divisional Ammunition Column April 1918		
War Diary	Souastre	02/04/1918	29/04/1918
War Diary	Souastre	14/04/1918	14/04/1918
War Diary	Henu	04/05/1918	15/05/1918
War Diary	Hamhoek	15/05/1918	04/06/1918
War Diary	Bambecque	06/06/1918	07/06/1918
War Diary	Zegger Cappel	08/06/1918	08/06/1918
War Diary	Buysscheure	09/06/1918	13/06/1918
War Diary	Ruminghem	20/06/1918	25/06/1918
War Diary	Zeggers Cappel	26/06/1918	26/06/1918
War Diary	L. 15.b.9.2.	01/07/1918	31/08/1918
War Diary	K.21.c.6.4.	01/09/1918	29/09/1918
War Diary		01/10/1918	31/10/1918
War Diary	Sheet 29	02/11/1918	13/11/1918
War Diary	Sheet 30	14/11/1918	29/11/1918
War Diary	Schendelbeke	11/12/1918	25/12/1918
War Diary	Burdinne	12/01/1919	12/01/1919
War Diary	Cologne	12/01/1919	12/01/1919
War Diary	Cologne	01/02/1919	28/02/1919
War Diary	Westhoven	06/03/1919	06/03/1919
War Diary	Germany	12/03/1919	22/03/1919
War Diary	Germany	01/03/1919	31/03/1919
War Diary	Germany	26/03/1919	26/03/1919
War Diary	Westhoven Germany	01/04/1919	30/04/1919
War Diary		26/04/1919	26/04/1919
War Diary	Westhoven	30/05/1919	30/05/1919
War Diary	Germany.	01/05/1919	31/05/1919
War Diary	Westhoven Germany	10/06/1919	10/06/1919
War Diary	Germany	13/06/1919	30/06/1919
War Diary		01/06/1919	30/06/1919
War Diary	Westhoven Germany	14/07/1919	14/07/1919
War Diary	Germany	17/07/1919	31/07/1919
War Diary	Westhoven	11/08/1919	11/08/1919
War Diary	Germany	11/08/1919	30/08/1919
War Diary		01/08/1919	31/08/1919

War Diary		01/08/1919	28/08/1919
War Diary	Westhoven Germany	01/09/1919	30/09/1919
War Diary		29/09/1919	30/09/1919

WO 95/2025/11
41 DIV
DIV AMM'N COLUMN   MARCH 1918
                   - SEPT 1919

Army Form C. 2118

WAR DIARY
or
INTELLIGENCE SUMMARY
(Erase heading not required.)

41 st D.A.C. R.F.A.

Vol 23

Place	Date	Hour	Summary of Events and Information	Remarks and references to Appendices
VEDELAGO	5.3.18	—	D.A.C. marched to CASTAGNOLE.	
CASTAGNOLE	6.3.18	—	D.A.C. Re-organised. Became H.Q, No1 Sec, No2 Sec, + SAA Section. Surplus Personnel Animals Equipm to 48 DAC	
"	7.3.18	—	Marched to TREVISO + entrained for FRANCE.	
In Train	10.3.18	—	Portion of No1 Sec detrained at DOULLENS.	
"	11.3.18	—	Remainder of D.A.C. detrained at DOULLENS + moved into Billets at H.Q + No 2 Sec GROUCHES, No 1 Sec MILLY	
Billets nr DOULLENS	12.3.18	—	S.A.A Section at BOUT-des-TRES.	
"	21.3.18	—	D.A.C. held in Readiness to entrain at 24 hours notice.	
Mollens-au-Bois	22.3.18	—	Marched to Billets at MOLLIENS-AU-BOIS.	
		—	Marched to Bivouacs nr ACHIET-LE-GRAND. Sleep at LENS J.5.45.70. Forced march about 35 mile. Guns went straight into action	
Achiet-le-Grand	23.3.18	—	at FAVREUIL RIDGE. D.A.C were delivering Ammn to G guns all night.	
Achiet-le-Petit	24.3.18	—	Retired to ACHIET-LE-PETIT J.5.16.	
Bucquoy	24/25.3.18	—	Retired to Bucquoy Sh.57 D. L.9.6.5.8.	
		—	Retired at Midnight 24/25 to N. ESSARTS. F.25.6.2.9.	
N. Essarts	25.3.18	—	Retired a 2 m in G Bivouac at SOUASTRE D.21.6.5.1.	
Souastre	26.3.18	—	Moved to BERLES-AU-BOIS Sh 11. LENS H.4.5.2.	
Berles-au-Bois	27.3.18	—	Moved to SOUASTRE Sh.57 D. D.21.6.5.1. 1 Horse No 2 Sec Killed by shell fire.	
Souastre	28.3.18	—	SAA Section moved to GAUDIEMPRE Sh.57 D. D.1.6. This Section to detailed for work with Div. Infantry.	
"	29.3.18	—	S.A.A Section moved to COUIN J.1.6.	
			From 21st to end of month every vehicle of the D.A.C. was employed day + night drawing Ammunition from Railhead + delivering to batteries.	

31/3/18

A.R. Hurst Lt Col. RFA
Commanding 41 D.A.C. R.F.A

41st Divisional Artillery

WAR DIARY

41st DIVISIONAL AMMUNITION COLUMN

APRIL 1918

WAR DIARY
INTELLIGENCE SUMMARY

Army Form C. 2118

41st D.A.C. R.F.A.

Place	Date	Hour	Summary of Events and Information	Remarks and references to Appendices
SOUASTRE	2.4.18	—	SAA Section marched to FAMECHON. Map Ref Sh 57.D C 26.6.	
	3.4.18	—	SAA Section entrained at PETIT HOUVIN. Sh LENS H.D.3 8.9.	
	4.4.18	—	SAA Section detrained at CROMBEKE marched to Camp at HAMADEK STANDINGS Sh HAZEBROUCK I.2.6.4.	
	6.4.18	—	3 Horses No 1 Sec wounded.	
	21.4.18	—	VAR & No 1 Sec moved to new Bivouac at Sh 57.D 20 a. owing to hostile H.V. Shelling & property practice setting grant.	
	25.4.18	—	SAA Section moved to A 29 Central Sheet 28. No 60408 F LOVETT wounded hand.	
	29.4.18	—	Lt E.H. BINDLOSS posted to Command SAA Section vice Major R. REARDON to A/93 A.F.A.	
	30.4.18	—	The whole month No 1 & 2 Sec have been kept very busy supplying Ammunition to Batteries (strong parties of Gunners at A.R.Ps.) on the 21st Inst. the B. MG. to which No 1 Sec is affiliated were withdrawn for refit consequently relieving the work of No 1 Sec somewhat.	

The SAA Section accompanied the 41st Division up North to work in conjunction with the Infantry. They have been very hard worked drawing & supplying Mileno of R's of SAA & Flares etc to Engineer Fatigue, Salvage work, practically, having all wagons & teams out DAILY.

Many Reinforcements, Officers & OR's have passed through the unit & sent on to Brigades, during the month.

1/5/18

J.R. Revel
Lt. Col. R.F.A.
Comdg. 41 D.A.C. R.F.A.

Army Form C. 2118

WAR DIARY
or
INTELLIGENCE SUMMARY   41st DAC RFA
(Erase heading not required.)

Instructions regarding War Diaries and Intelligence Summaries are contained in F.S. Regs, Part II. and the Staff Manual respectively. Title Pages will be prepared in manuscript.

Place	Date	Hour	Summary of Events and Information	Remarks and references to Appendices
HEN D	4.5.18	—	No. 2 Sec. moved to Sh. 57.D.C.22. d.5.8 on account of Hostile Shelling of Bivouac	
	7.5.18	—	No.1 Sec. attached to N.Z.D.A. Took over Dump D.20.6.0.6. Sh. 57.D also Reserve Gun Dumps.	
	13.5.18	—	No. 1 Sec. Handed over Dumps to 57 DAC.	
	14/5/18	—		
	15/5/18	—	HQ, No.1 & No.2 Sec. marched by Road to DOULLENS & entrained. Proceeded North detraining at NAAYENBURG SIDING BELGIUM Sh 19 X 19.a.4.9. & marched into Bivouac at LOVIE AERODROME Sh. 27.F.17.c. Central.	
HAMHOEK	17/5/18	—	HQ marched to Stables at HAMHOEK Sh. 28 A 25.6.0.8. No.1 Sec. Sh 27 F.24.a.9.4. No 2 Sec F.24.c.9.7. SAA Sec. came under the direct orders of O/C DAC. again.	
	19/5/18	—	Salvage Party under 2nd Moxon commenced work. Gun Commanders away	
	20/5/18	—	Instructional Classes for 41 DA Commenced. 8 N.C.O.s from Batteries Attended 1 Signal & 5 D.M.C. drivers of DAC & second Signal being trained as Gunners. Had loan of Spar Gun from A/157.	
	26/5/18	—	1 Rank No 2 Sec Killed whilst on Fatigue near YPRES.	
	29/5/18	—	1 Rank HQ wounded by A.A.-Aircraft fire.	
	30/5/18	—	1 Rank SAA Sec wounded J.S.M. No. 156214 G/A OLDCORN Remained at Duty. Ammunition supplied direct to Batteries largely by Light Railway under the direction of J.2 Lough MGC.	
			Heavy Air & Y Rain prevented pavan throughput DAC during the month. Engine Trains on Fatigues carting RE material to & from line	

16/18.

A R Kent
Lt Col R.F.A.
Commanding 41 DAC R.F.A.

WAR DIARY or INTELLIGENCE SUMMARY

Army Form C. 2118

41st D.A.C. R.F.A.

Vol 26

Place	Date	Hour	Summary of Events and Information	Remarks and references to Appendices
HAMHOEK	3.6.18	—	S.A.A. Sec. moved to ZEGGERS CAPPEL Sh. 27.B Central	
	4.6.18	—	S.A.A. continued march to 2nd Army Training area to BUYSSCHEURE Sh. HAZEBROUCK 5A D.3. 9.5. 1 mule & 1 Sec. wounded.	
BAMBECQUE	6.6.18	—	HQ. No 1 Sec. No 2 Sec. marched to BAMBECQUE Sh. 5A G.2.	
	7.6.18	—	HQ No 1 & 2 Sec. marched to ZEGGERS CAPPEL	
ZEGGER CAPPEL	8.6.18	—	HQ No 1 & 2 Sec. marched to Billets at RUMINGHEM Sh. 5A B.2.	
BUYSSCHEURE	9.6.18	—	S.A.A. rejoined DAC at RUMINGHEM	
	10.6.18	—	Commencement of Intensive Training of all Ranks.	
RUMINGHEM	20.6.18	—	Reorganisation of Nos 1 & 2 Sec. Reduction Teams of all Q.F. wagons from 6 to 4 Animals. Increased Spare Animals E/12, also 30 Drivers Surplus.	
	24.6.18	—	Inspection of DAC by 2nd Army Commander (General PLUMER). Surplus Personnel & Animals absorbed in units of 41 Division. Training Ends.	
	25.6.18	—	DAC marched to ZEGGERS CAPPEL	
ZEGGERS CAPPEL	26.6.18	—	DAC marched by night to Reserve at H.R. No 1 & 2 Sec. at Sh. 27 L.15.6.9.2. & S.A.A Sec. to WATOU FRANCE FARM Sh. 27. K.21. d.7.3.	

The programme of Training consists of; 36 Teams driving drill, 6 Rides, 5 Squads gun drill, 3 Officers Patrols daily in addition to Fatigues &c. 2 Route Marches 10 miles weekly.

On arriving in Reserve DAC very active Receiving Ammn from Rail Park & issuing to new Battery positions

During the month a sort of Influenza has been rampant in the Unit the High Temperature accompanying it Rendering the men unfit for Duty. Towards the end of month the epidemic showed signs of abating.

30/6/18

[signed] R.F. Hereward Lt Col R.F.A.
Commdg. 41 DAC R.F.A.

Army Form C. 2118

WAR DIARY or INTELLIGENCE SUMMARY
(Erase heading not required.)

41st DAC. RFA

Vol 27

Place	Date	Hour	Summary of Events and Information	Remarks and references to Appendices
L.15.6.9.2	1.7.18	—	1 Mule Killed & 1 Mule Wounded in Front Line S A A Section	
	2.7.18	—	H.Q. & No.1 Sec. marched to Bivouac K29.c.9.2. Dump formed at K.34.6.	
	3.7.18	—	J.R. moved to K.36.a.4.2. No.2 Sec K.35.d.6.4.	
	5.7.18	—	H.Q. moved to K.21.c.6.4.	
	6.7.18	—	Section & Animals Inspected by Divisional Commander.	
	7.7.18	—	New A.R.P. formed at K.27.a.5.3.	
	10.7.18	—	New A.R.P. formed at STEEN AKKER R.2.b.4.6. (Sh.27).	
	17.7.18	—	Reserve Dump established at BEAUVOORDE South K.21.C.4.0.	
	18.7.18	—	Enemy Aircraft bombed No. 2 Sec Bivouac. Dr. DABURN (no 4/46255) Killed. 14 Mules Killed & 21 Wounded.	

All this month the DAC has been very Busy in the Front Line Making New Gun Positions
Cable Burying, taking up Ammunition to New forward positions & Bringing Back Salvaged
Ammunition & ration & material of all sorts.

As all this work in addition to keeping the Artillery of the Division supplied were
personnel than can be found in the DAC assistance was given by the 158 Army B. R.F.A.
& the 66th Division who were temporarily attached to the DAC.

A R Hirst
Lt Col R.F.A.
1/8/18   Commanding 41 DAC RFA

Army Form C. 2118

WAR DIARY
INTELLIGENCE SUMMARY
(Erase heading not required.)

41st D.A.C. R.F.A.

WR 28

Instructions regarding War Diaries and Intelligence Summaries are contained in F. S. Regs., Part II. and the Staff Manual respectively. Title Pages will be prepared in manuscript.

Place	Date	Hour	Summary of Events and Information	Remarks and references to Appendices
SAME LOCATIONS	1-9 8/18	—	Nil	
	10.8.18	—	1 Mule Killed & 2 Wounded S.A.A. Sec.	
	11-16 8/18	—	Nil	
	17.8.18	—	Reserve Dump for E Poperinghe Line taken over from 66th D.A.C. Located at Sh.28/K.22.a.5.2.	
	18-27 8/18	—	Nil	
	28.8.18	—	Evans' Dump 27/L.33.d.3.5. taken over from 66th D.A.C.	
	29.8.18	—	S.A.A. Sec. marched to RENESCURE 27/T.20.d. to Bivouac.	
	30.8.18	—	S.A.A. Sec. continued march to TILQUES. Sh. HAZEBROUCK 5A. 3.C.5.B.	
	31.8.18	—	Nil	

During the month in addition to carrying Ammunition to the Gun Line both by Pack & Wagon approximately 10,000 Rds Gun Ammunition have been collected by the D.A.C. sorted and disposed of according to Corps Orders. The Amm'n that has been abandoned during withdrawal in April '18 & now permanent Ammunition Dump has been completed at STEENWERKE 27/K.2.6.4.6 and assistance given to the Royal Engineers & Infantry in getting ambulance forward to the Trench Sys Coms.

31.8.18

[signature] Lt. Col. R.F.A.
Commanding 41 D.A.C. R.F.A.

WAR DIARY
or
INTELLIGENCE SUMMARY

(Erase heading not required.)

Army Form C. 2118

41st D.A.C. R.F.A.

Place	Date	Hour	Summary of Events and Information	Remarks and references to Appendices
K.21.c.6.4.	1/9/18		Nil	
	2-9-18		H.Q. moved to K.32.d.2.0. No.1 Sect moved to G.33.c.7085. No.2 Sect moved to G.33.b central	
	3-9-18		S.A.A. Section arrived K.18.d.3.4.	
	4-9-18		H.Q. moved to G.33.a.6.8. EVANS & STEENAKKER DUMPS cleared to ROBSON DUMP	
	5-9-18		A.R.P. in K.22.a.5.2. cleared	
	8-9-18		H.Q. moved L.23.6.4.9. No.1 Sect L.22.6.4.8. No.2 Section to L.16.2.5-8	
	15-9-18		H.Q. moved to G.20.C.3.8. No.1 Sect. to G.26.a.9.1.	
	17-9-18		No.2 Section moved to G.25.6.3.3. "	
	24-9-18		Commencement of training of Mounted Patrol	
			ROBSON DUMP cleared to BEATTY DUMP	
	25-9-18		H.Q. moved to G.26.d.8.2. No.1 Section to G.34.6.5-5 No.2 Section to G.34.6.3.8.	
			H.Q. moved to H.27.6.7.7. No.1 Section to H.28.d.1.2. No.2 Section to H.22.d.6.3.	
	29.9.18		S.A.A. Section & had horses killed by shell fire	

All this month 41st D.A.C. were making preparations for the battle which commenced on the 28th. Fascines & trench bridges were got up by night to enable the guns to get forward as quickly as possible. Ammunition Dumps were completed & all possible assistance given to the Royal Engineers in transporting material for the Infantry. A fighting patrol of 15 selected N.C.O's & men was formed by order of the G.O.C. & came under the orders of the G.O.C. 41st Division for the battle commencing on the 28th & the subsequent operations. During the first week of this month 18 pdrs and 3 4.5" Hows. occupied in the Div. Area were brought in to our lines by the D.A.C.

R.R. Finch Lt. Col.
Comdg. 41st D.A.C. R.F.A.

WAR DIARY or INTELLIGENCE SUMMARY

Army Form C. 2118

41st D.A.C. R.F.A.

Vol 50

Place	Date	Hour	Summary of Events and Information	Remarks and references to Appendices
	1-10-18		H.Q. & No 1 & 2 Sections moved to lines between VOORMEZEELE & LOCK 8	
	7-10-18		Forward lines formed at GELUWELT for Q.F. Waggons. Indian Personnel arrived.	
	10-10-18		S.A.A. Section had two mules killed by shell fire	
	12-10-18		H.Q. & No 1 Section marched to 28/T.11.a.2.8. 3 Indians killed & 4 wounded by hostile shellfire.	
	14-10-18		H.Q. & No 1 Section marched to 29/J.29.G.6.1.	
	17-10-18		H.Q. & No 1 Section marched to 28/Z.15.d.0.3. No 2 Section to 28/L.22.a.55. SAA to 28/K.17.6.25	
	18-10-18		S.A.A. Section marched /15 28/L.16.a.2.3.	
	19-10-18		Dump & Q.F. Waggons marched to G.21.d. (Sheet 29)	
	20-10-18		S.A.A. Section marched to 29/ G.35.a.5.7. No 2 Section to 29/G.36.c.9.6. A.R.P. &G.35d.1.9.	
	21-10-18		H.Q. & No 1 Section marched to 29/M.8.6.9.5. No 2 Section to 29/H.33.c.1.11.	
	25-10-18		H.Q marched to 29/H.34.c.7.3. No 1 Section to 29/H. 33 Central. No 2 Section to 29/H.33.c.1.11.	
			L Indians (SAA Section) wounded.	
	27-10-18		H.Q. Marched to COURTRAI	
	30-10-18		New A.R.P. formed at 29/I.31-c-11.	
	31-10-18		Inspection of Sections by G.O.C. 41 DIVISION.	

This month saw the advance of the 41st Division. 19th Corps, to the SCHELDT, the LYS being crossed on pontoons on the 21st. The C.R.A. adopted the system of advancing the Q.F. Waggons of the D.A.C. in close support of the batteries, moving up the Q.F. reserve wagons to forward H.Qs. as soon as vacated. The S.A.A. section were advanced in the same method by direct orders from the "Q" Branch, in close support of the infantry. The guns were kept fully supplied with ammunition & the system adopted works excellently.

31/10/18

R. Kerr Lt Col
Comg. 41 D.A.C.

Army Form C. 2118

WAR DIARY or INTELLIGENCE SUMMARY

(Erase heading not required.)

41st D.A.C. R.F.A.

Vol 31

Place	Date	Hour	Summary of Events and Information	Remarks and references to Appendices
SHEET 29	2.11.18		H.Q. moved to O.9.c.5.2, No 1 & 2 to O.2.6, S.A.A. to O.6.6, A.R.P. at O.W.6. (Sheet 29)	
	4.11.18		H.Q. moved with No 1 & S.A.A. Sect. to I.20.6. No 2 Sect. to I.20.a. A.R.P. at O.W.6 handed over	
	8.11.18		Dump at J.25.d.8.3 taken over	
	10.11.18		H.Q. moved to P.6.d.8-9, No 1 & P.12.b.4.4. No 2 to Q.7.a.1.2. A.R.P. to Q.15.a.8.9	
	11.11.18		HOSTILITIES CEASED at 11 a.m.	
	12.11.18		H.Q. moved to Q.21.6.5.5. No 1 to Q.21.d.4.6 S.A.A.Sect. to Q.9.c.1.6	
	13.11.18		No 2 Sect moved to Q.21.a.4.5	
SHEET 30	14.11.18		H.Q. moved to N.20.b.2.2, No 1 to N.21.c.2.0, No 2 to N.13.d.5.5, S.A.A. to N.20.a.7.2	
	15.11.18		H.Q. moved to P.22.a.2.5 No 1 to P.17.c.4.0. No 2 & S.A.A.Sect. to P.16.c.3.2. 11 BAC to P.21.a.4.7	
	26.11.18		Distribution of medals & awards by G.O.C. 41 DIV.	
	29.11.18		41 D.A.C. & 11 B.A.C. inspected by G.O.C. R.A.	
			After the crossing of the SCHELDT by the 41st DIV. on the 12th, the owing to the bridges being unfit for motor transport the D.A.C. Supplies 30 wagons daily to the Brit. train for the transport of supplies. The Army Education Scheme was discussed & preparations were made to carry it out during our stay in winter quarters.	

30/11/18

Chas Jn Kenrick Capt. R.F.A.

Comdg 41 D.A.C. R.F.A.

Army Form C. 2118

WAR DIARY or INTELLIGENCE SUMMARY

(Erase heading not required.)

41st D.A.C. R.F.A.

Place	Date	Hour	Summary of Events and Information	Remarks and references to Appendices
SCHENDELBEKE	11th		Distribution of decorations by G.O.C. 41st DIV. at GRAMMONT. ※	※ RECIPIENTS: FRENCH CROIX-de-GUERRE: Major E.W.BURDROSS M.C. T/Capt. C. KENRICK 201610 Sgt DANIELS 60565 Bdr RICHARDS 700082 Dr TAYLOR L/1040 Sgt LITTLEJOHN L/40071 Sgt BIGBY L/1206 Gnr MYERS.
	12		41 D.A.C. marched to MOERBEKE village.	
	13		41 D.A.C. marched to TUBIZE area.	
	14		41 D.A.C. marched to BRAINE LE CHATEAU	
	16		41 D.A.C. Marched to MONT ST PONT.	
	17		41 D.A.C. Marched to QUATRE BRAS area & HOUTAIN LE VAL.	
	18		41 D.A.C. Marched to BOIGNEE area.	
	19		41 D.A.C. Marched to HANRET area	
	20		H.Q., No.2 Sect. & S.A.A. Sect. marched to quarters in BURDINNE. No.1 Sect. to BOING.	
	25		First batch of men, 18 miners, despatched to U.K.	
			During this month the 115th A.F.A. B.A.C. were placed under the orders of O.C. 41 D.A.C. & marched as an section of the D.A.C. under D.R.O. No. 1035 dated 29/12/19 the M.M. was awarded to the following O.R.s of the 41st D.A.C.: - L/44645 Dr WORMS E.W. 461143 Sgt FORSYTH.R. L/4965 Corpl KERR. H.R. 47234 Dvr. SHORT. H. 28748 Corpl LAWRENCE C. 37157 Sgt SMITH. W.G.	

31/12/18

A. R. Hurst, Lt. Col.
Comdg. 41 D.A.C. R.F.A.

WAR DIARY
or
INTELLIGENCE SUMMARY

(Erase heading not required.)

Army Form C. 2118

Vol 55
41st D.A.C.

Place	Date	Hour	Summary of Events and Information	Remarks and references to Appendices
BURDINNE	12/19		From 1st to 12th January the 41st D.A.C. were retained at BURDINNE, BELGIUM. (17 kilos from HUY) about midway between LIÈGE & NAMUR. Visits by lorry were arranged for parties of Officers, N.C.O's men & to the Cathl places. D.A.C. Entrained in Sections at Huy & ANDENNE for the purpose of proceeding to Germany, to join 2nd Army (Army of Occupation). Three sections with a person of 180 days detrained at WAHN, and marched to billets at	
COLOGNE			WESTHOVEN on the RHINE about 5 miles from COLOGNE. N.C.O's & Men continue to be despatched in small numbers for Demobilization. 11th B.A.C. did not move with 41st D.A.C. The undermentioned were granted the Belgian Croix de Guerre T/Lt. (A/capt) S.A. Inkham R.F.A. 13619 Cpl Latham W. 1589 Spr (A/3 Q.M.S) S Bonny S.1.1.19 13619 the M.S.M. was awarded to L/044606 Dr W.W. Holmes London Gazette 18.1.19 31/1/19	

R R Kennet Lt Col
Commdg 41st D.A.C. R.F.A.

Army Form C. 2118

WAR DIARY

~~INTELLIGENCE SUMMARY~~

(Erase heading not required.)

41st D.A.C. R.F.A.

Vol 34

Instructions regarding War Diaries and Intelligence Summaries are contained in F. S. Regs., Part II. and the Staff Manual respectively. Title Pages will be prepared in manuscript.

Place	Date	Hour	Summary of Events and Information	Remarks and references to Appendices
COLOGNE	1.2.19 to 28.2.19		During the whole of the month the D.A.C. has remained at Westhoven on the Rhine. On the 12th, demobilization was temporarily suspended pending the arrival of reinforcements, the strength of the D.A.C. having fallen to minimum laid down by G.R.A. Ammunition has been stored under cover, cleaned and sorted. A new establishment of ammunition (by natures & fuzes) having been laid down by Army authority.	
	28.2.19		A.Ritchie Lieut. Col. R.F.A. Commanding 41st D.A.C. R.F.A.	

1875 Wt. W593/826 1,000,000 4/15 J.B.C. & A. A.D.S.S./Forms/C. 2118.

Army Form C. 2118

WAR DIARY
or
INTELLIGENCE SUMMARY   London D.A.C. R.F.A.
(Erase heading not required.)

Instructions regarding War Diaries and Intelligence Summaries are contained in F. S. Regs., Part II. and the Staff Manual respectively. Title Pages will be prepared in manuscript.

Place	Date	Hour	Summary of Events and Information	Remarks and references to Appendices
Westhoven	6/3/19		Lieut. Col. J.P.D. Wheatley, T.D. R.F.A. assumed command of 41st Divisional Ammunition Column vice Lt Col. A.R. Hurst, DSO. RFA. Demobilized	
Germany	19/3/19		In consequence of the change of designation of 41st Division to London Division, the 41st D.A.C. will in future be known as London Div. Amm. Column.	
	22/3/19		Inspection of Sections by G.O.C. London Division, and presentation of medal ribbons to NCOs' Men	
	from 1/3/19 to 31/3/19		Some of the gun ammunition removed by the Sections to the Fort at Westhoven. Demobilization almost at a standstill. During the whole of the month the D.A.C. has remained at Westhoven on the Rhine.	
	26/3/19		Inspection of Sections by Brigadier General L.L.L. Oldfield, C.M.G. D.S.O. on assuming command of London Div. Artillery	

31/3/19

J.W. Wheatley
Lieut. Col. R.F.A.
Commanding London D.A.C.

Army Form C. 2118

WAR DIARY
or
INTELLIGENCE SUMMARY

London D.A.C. R.F.A.

(Erase heading not required.)

Instructions regarding War Diaries and Intelligence Summaries are contained in F. S. Regs., Part II. and the Staff Manual respectively. Title Pages will be prepared in manuscript.

Place	Date	Hour	Summary of Events and Information	Remarks and references to Appendices
Beethoven Germany	1/7/19 to 30/7/19		During the whole of the month the D.A.C. has remained at Beethoven on the Rhine. All Gun ammunition has now been removed to the Forts at Beethoven. Demobilization almost at a standstill, owing to non arrival of reinforcements.	
	26/7/19	10 A.M.	G.R.A. inspected 1 Officer 1 Sgt and 1 18 pdr Q.F. Wagon and team in Field Service Marching Order with a view to standardizing the packing & carrying of Equipment.	

30/7/19

J.P.D. Wheatley
Lieut Col. R.F.A.
Commanding London D.A.C.

Army Form C. 2118

AMMUNITION COLUMN. London Divisional
27/37

WAR DIARY
or
INTELLIGENCE SUMMARY
(Erase heading not required.)

London R.F.A.

Place	Date	Hour	Summary of Events and Information	Remarks and references to Appendices
Westham	30/7	10.00	L.R.Q. London Division inspected the D.A.C. in Field Service Marching Order.	
Germany	1/19 to 31/5/19		All Ammunition removed from Fort 86, and placed in Wagons, in case of emergency. The D.A.C. remained at Westhoven, all the month. Nearly all men for demobilization sent to England. A conference of officers rolo on the "Housing Question" in England & Wales, as requested by the War Office, was held at Westhoven on the 30 5/1/9, when it was unanimously decided in favour of the Government proposal, same decision being forwarded to London D.A. for information of Local Government Board.	
	6/1/19			

J.W. Wheatley
Lt. Col. R.F.A.
Commanding London D.A.C.

Army Form C. 2118

WAR DIARY
or
INTELLIGENCE SUMMARY
(Erase heading not required.)

London D.A.C.   June 1919

Instructions regarding War Diaries and Intelligence Summaries are contained in F. S. Regs., Part II. and the Staff Manual respectively. Title Pages will be prepared in manuscript.

Place	Date	Hour	Summary of Events and Information	Remarks and references to Appendices
Beethoven	10/6/19		Corps Commander inspected the D.A.C. He expressed his satisfaction with the turn out.	
Germany	13/6/19		Lieut. A/Capt. J. Pepen died at 36 C.C.S. of Influenza	
	18/6/19		The S.A.A. Section of the D.A.C. joined the 3rd London Infantry Bde. for the purpose of advancing in the event of Germany not signing the Peace Terms.	
	28/6/19		Germany signed the Peace Terms.	
	30/6/19		S.A.A. Section rejoined the D.A.C. at Beethoven.	
	1/6/19 to 30/6/19		All Infantry attached to the D.A.C. rejoined their units. Headquarters, No. 1 & 2 Sections remained at Beethoven on the Rhine.	

J.D. Wheatley
Lieut. Col. R.F.A.
Commanding London D.A.C.

Army Form C. 2118

War Diary A

INTELLIGENCE SUMMARY

(Erase heading not required.)

London D.A.C.

July 1919

Instructions regarding War Diaries and Intelligence Summaries are contained in F. S. Regs., Part II. and the Staff Manual respectively. Title Pages will be prepared in manuscript.

Place	Date	Hour	Summary of Events and Information	Remarks and references to Appendices
Sulthorn Germany	10th July 14th		L.R.C. Khan Army visited D.A.C. L.R.A. London horses inspected and on field day and front Post 100 N.C.O's & Men L.D.A attached for duty	
	"	1.30 to 3.30	D.A.C. remained at Sulthorn on the Rhine	

1/7 A954

J. J. Taylor

Lt. J. Taylor, Capt. R.F.A.
Commanding London D.A.C.

Army Form C. 2118

WAR DIARY
or
INTELLIGENCE SUMMARY

AUGUST 1919 London L.A.C.

Place	Date	Hour	Summary of Events and Information	Remarks and references to Appendices
Westhoven	11.		Capt Ilsley R.F.A. L.A.A section admitted to Hospital with Concussion (severe) the happened while exercising / jumping with a horse.	
Germany	24.		L.A.C. held Mounted Sports at Westhoven under the patronage of Lt Col L.L.J. London Lennon who expressed appreciation of LS turn out.	
	30		1 Officer sensibility also a few Compassionate cases.	
	1st to 31st		L.A.C. remained at Westhoven.	

September 1st 1919.

J.W. Wheatley
Lieut Colonel R.F.A.
L.A.C. R.F.17
London
Commanding London L.A.C.

War Diary.

Month of August.   PLACE - BRÜCH

2ND LONDON BDE.
LIGHT TRENCH
MORTAR BATTERY
No. TM/A359
DATE 1-9-19

DATE	DAY	
1st	Friday	Musketry, Specialist Training and Education were carried out.
2nd	Saturday	General Training and Interior Economy.
4th	Monday (BANK HOLIDAY)	No military training was carried out. Cricket match v. 2nd London Inf. Bde.
5th	Tuesday	Musketry, Education and Trench Mortar training, the last, taking the form of a practice Shoot.
6th	Wednesday	Drill & Educational Training
7th	Thursday	Musketry, Trench Mortar Training and Education.
8th	Friday	} Education Demonstration Class for Method Course, held near London Divisional Reception Camp, Cologne-Deutz.
9th	Saturday	
11th	Monday	
12th	Tuesday	
13th	Wednesday	
14th	Thursday	
15th	Friday	Educational, Musketry, Trench Mortar Training and General Training were carried out. Cricket match v "2/4th Queen's".
16th	Saturday	Educational Training; a Kit, Billet & Transport inspection was held.
18th	Monday	Drill, Education, Musketry and Trench Mortar Training.
19th	Tuesday	Drill, Education, & Trench Mortar Training were carried out. Also a tug-of-war contest with Lond. Divisional Signallers, in which the L.T.M. Battery was unsuccessful.
20th	Wednesday	Education, Drill and Musketry practice.
21st	Thursday	General Training, Education, and Trench Mortar Practice (Theory) were carried out.
22nd	Friday	Education, Musketry and Drill.
23rd	Saturday	Educational & Musketry Training. A Billet & Kit Inspection was held.
25th	Monday	Drill, Musketry & Education. T.M. Training.
26th	Tuesday	General & Trench Mortar Training.
27th	Wednesday	Educational & Physical Training: Musketry Practice.
28th	Thursday	Drill, Musketry & Trench Mortar Training.

Army Form C. 2118

WAR DIARY
or
INTELLIGENCE SUMMARY
(Erase heading not required.)

September 1919   London D.A.C.

Instructions regarding War Diaries and Intelligence Summaries are contained in F. S. Regs., Part II. and the Staff Manual respectively. Title Pages will be prepared in manuscript.

Place	Date	Hour	Summary of Events and Information	Remarks and references to Appendices
Westhoven Germany	1st to 30.9.		Demobilization and leave cancelled owing to Railway strike in England. D.a.c. remained at Westhoven during Sept 1919. 10/79.	

J.M.Wheatley
LIEUT. COL. R. F. A.
COMMANDING LONDON D.A.C. R.F.A.

War Diary (Contd.)

DATE	DAY	
29th	Friday	Education, Drill & Musketry Practice.
30th	Saturday	Educational Training and Interior Economy. An inspection of Billets & Kits was held.

BRÜCK
1-9-19

[signature]
....CAPT.
CMDG. 2nd LONDON L.T.M. BATTERY

www.ingramcontent.com/pod-product-compliance
Lightning Source LLC
Chambersburg PA
CBHW081251170426
43191CB00037B/2120